THE CFL SHITSHOW INTO XFL PIPE DREAM LAND:

IN DEFENCE OF CANADIAN FOOTBALL DURING THE PANDEMIC

John Mackenzie

Agora Books

Agora Books™
Ottawa, Canada

The CFL Shitshow into XFL Pipe Dream Land: In defence of Canadian football during the pandemic

© 2021, John Mackenzie

Agora Books_{TM}
P.O. Box 24191
300 Eagleson Road
Kanata, Ontario K2M 2C3 CANADA

Agora Books is a self-publishing agency for authors that was launched by The Agora Cosmopolitan which is a registered not-for-profit corporation.

ISBN: 978-1-927538-41-8

Printed in Canada

Contents

Canadian football has an illustrious history and a bright future as an expression of our national identity. But the great potential of that bright future can never be realized with short-sightedness.

Professional leagues across North America have shown that with creativity and determination, it is possible to survive and develop during a pandemic without selling out or tarnishing the reputations of their leagues. The proposed partnership between the Canadian Football League (CFL) and the Xtreme Football League (XFL) would mean nothing less than Canadian football selling its soul. The merger with the doomed American league represents a betrayal of all the sacrifices that Canadians have made in the effort to grow and preserve the unique, vibrant football culture that the CFL represents.

Grey Cup celebrations in the CFL have become an expression of the dynamic of east versus west that is pivotal to our cultural roots and our national destiny. Indeed, Canada forged itself as a nation on the determination to unite our eastern and western regions. The CFL was conceived by the same east-west inspiration. There is no other Canadian professional competition at the same level of quality and prestige, or which similarly represents a celebration of Canada itself. Only the CFL and the Grey Cup occupy this role. Therefore, to contemplate selling out the CFL for the illusion of wealth promised by a league that has no successful seasons to its name would be a catastrophic mistake and an epic betrayal.

The CFL is more than a professional sports league, just as the Grey Cup has never been simply a Canadian version of the Superbowl. The CFL, and the unique football culture it represents, is an expression of our national heritage. We must reject the talks among league owners that contemplate variations of assimilation into American football; such changes would destroy the CFL as a national institution. Watering down Canadian football is as unthinkable as the incorporation of Canada as a 51st American state.

This book explores the incompetence that the CFL has shown in its publicized talks with the XFL. *The CFL Shitshow in XFL Pipe Dream Land* hopes to inspire the kind of creative thinking and public debate among fans of Canadian football that will wake the CFL out of its sleepwalk toward destruction. Partnership with the XFL would inevitably destroy the mix of rules that are pivotal to Canadian football as it is played in high schools, universities, and colleges across Canada. Together we can work to prevent this catastrophe.

CFL: 8 reasons Randy Ambrosie needs to resign as Commissioner–Stop the Shitshow!

THIS TIME CFL COMMISSIONER RANDY Ambrosie has gone too far with the prevailing media-publicized talks of so-called "alignment" between the CFL and the XFL. Here are eight reasons why the best thing that Mr. Ambrosie could do to save football in Canada and rejuvenate the CFL is not his sought alignment with the XFL, but his immediate resignation as Commissioner:

1–Did Mr. Ambrosie professionally occupy a senior professional role in a sports operation like his immediate predecessor Commissioner Jerry Orridge?

In 1991, Mr. Orridge became head of business and legal affairs at USA Basketball,[1] the governing body for the Olympic sport, and in 1994, he joined Reebok International. In the mid-to-late 1990s, he became global sports marketing director for Reebok International,[2] and was sports licensing director for Warner Bros Consumer Products.

The apparent answer is NO! Mr. Ambrosie appears to lack such experience.

2–Did Mr. Ambrosie obtain experience as the successful General Manager or the President of a CFL club like Jake Gaudaur?

From 1954, Gaudaur was President of the Tiger-Cats and was President & General Manager from the 1956 season[3] to 1967.[4] The Ti-Cats appeared in 9 Grey Cups over his term as general manager and won in 1957,[5] 1963,[6] 1965,[7] and 1967.[8]

The answer is NO! Ambrosie does not appear to have any such General Manager or executive management experience of a CFL team and seems to have had only one Grey Cup win to his belt as a player.

3–Did Mr. Ambrosie serve as a board member of a successful Canadian corporation like John Tory who also served as Commissioner?

From 1995 to 1999, John Tory returned to Rogers Communications,[9] but this time as president and CEO of Rogers Media, which has become one of Canada's largest publishing and broadcasting companies.

The answer is NO!

4–Is Mr. Ambrosie a successful former Canadian politician or manager of a national political organization like former CFL Commissioners John Tory or Keith Davey?

From 1981 to 1985, Mr. Tory served in the office of the premier of Ontario[10] Bill Davis[11] as principal secretary[12] to the premier and associate secretary of the cabinet. After Davis retired as premier in 1985, Tory joined the office of the Canadian Special Envoy on Acid Rain[13] as a special advisor.

Davey directed the Liberal campaigns in 1962,[14] 1963,[15] and 1965.[16] Commuting regularly between homes in Ottawa and Toronto, Davey played important roles in every federal Liberal campaign through 1984, serving Prime Ministers Lester Pearson,[17] Pierre Trudeau,[18] and John Turner.[19]

The answer is NO!

5–Did Mr. Ambrosie develop organizational skills after having been a lawyer like former interim CFL Commissioner Jim Lawson?

A lawyer by profession, Mr. Lawson has been a partner at Torys LLP[20] and Davies Ward Phillips & Vineberg LLP.[21]

The answer is NO!

6–Did Mr. Ambrosie become CFL Commissioner after a successful tenure in sports marketing like Mark Cohon?

Before Cohon became CFL Commissioner, he worked at the NBA, as head of international marketing, and at Major League Baseball International, as head of corporate development, before becoming President and chief executive officer of Audience View Ticketing,[22] a company that sells ticketing systems and services to sports, arts, and entertainment events.

The answer in NO!

7–Surely, Mr. Ambrosie must have an extensive background in marketing and sales, which is a critical skill for a Commissioner when seeking to market a professional league like the CFL?

Former CFL Commissioner Keith Davey was a sales manager for CKFH,[23] a Toronto radio station, from 1949 to 1960 before he became linchpin organizer for the Liberal Party.

The answer is **somewhat limited.**

In May 2004, Mr. Ambrosie joined AGF Management Ltd. as their head of sales and marketing. In June 2006, Ambrosie was appointed president of AGF Funds, but due to another managerial change in 2008, Ambrosie left the firm. That's just four years with the company.

8–Was Mr. Ambrosie a successful entrepreneur who demonstrated a tremendous degree of financial success running various businesses in the financial services or other sectors like former CFL Commissioner Ted Workman?[24]

Former CFL Commissioner Ted Workman worked as a manager selection and asset allocation advisor for large institutional investors, including pension funds, university endowments, cooperatives, and retirement funds. He is the founder and developer of Performex, a proprietary investment analytical system.

The answer is NO!

It is apparent that Mr Ambrosie is totally in over his head. Most of the time, he looks like a deer caught in the headlights since the pandemic began, and you can easily see why from his publicized résumé. He simply lacks the experience of his predecessors, and all the so-called professional sports journalists who ignore this fact in their coverage of CFL woes during the pandemic *are complicit.*

Randy Ambrosie has failed the CFL on leadership during the pandemic because he simply lacks the breadth of experience of other such Commissioners of the CFL before him, or of his counterparts in professional leagues that have been able to persevere during the pandemic.

Simply put, Mr. Ambrosie reminds me of the literary folktale "The Emperor's New Clothes." Arguably, Mr Ambrosie as CFL Commissioner is like giving someone who usually rides tricycles the job to pilot an airplane.

The Canadian Football League (CFL) is more than "guys getting paid to play football along with their owners." The CFL and the Grey Cup bring together a passionate clash between east and west at the heart of our national psyche. Canadians know this, but it is apparent that Randy Ambrosie is on the verge of surrendering our national psyche to an upstart league run by rednecks and Hollywood rabble rousers as a result of his incompetence or complicity in a "North American Union" (NAU) agenda.

The Grey Cup has been and is a celebration of who we are as Canadians, and the CFL is completely different than all the North American professional sports entities out there, which lack the soul of the CFL. The CFL celebrates the very communities that it has grown to represent.

Indeed, the CFL is older than Canada itself and the Grey Cup has been a national celebration bringing together East and West, above and beyond politics for generations, and now that idiot wants to sell-out our national treasure to an upstart sports league founded by rednecks which has been the butt of jokes by fans of the National Football League (NFL) in the United States?

These Canadian sports journalists who are apparently salivating at "The Rock" like school girls screaming at a boy band have absolutely no national pride in the traditions of our national game, and have allowed an arguably incompetent Commissioner to take OUR game to the brink of assimilation to the underbelly of Americana that XFL gimmickry represents.

XFL is a shallow league run by shallow people without the traditions of the CFL. The "reincarnated" XFL hasn't even played a game yet! But, alas, Ambrosie can't run a league like the CFL and now seems to want "The Rock" to run it for him? *What an outrage!*

Remember that dumb-ass expansion in the United States which almost destroyed the CFL? *Guess who was a part of that?* If you guessed Mr. Ambrosie, then you're right! Ambrosie was also part of the CFLPA board that oversaw the CFL's expansion into the United States.[25]

Canadian football fans who love our national game need to put a stop to Randy Ambrosie's shitshow and collectively demand his resignation in favour of a far more competent CFL Commissioner.

A competent CFL Commissioner during Spring 2020 would have been able to make football happen here, just like the NFL, and would have been able to do it at a time when there was a critical demand for live sports. This would have been possible by coordinating all Canadian lineups to fill-in for American players who were not able to cross the border — a difficult but not impossible task for a Commissioner with far greater professional experiences and creative talents.

The fact that the NFL, MLB, NHL and NBA did not need to totally cancel their seasons boils down to the lack of competence of the current presiding Commissioner of the CFL.

We need a Commissioner who is going to consolidate, expand, and celebrate OUR GAME, a Commissioner who will not destroy and assimilate it because he lacks the experience and vision to be the Commissioner of the CFL.

The number of Canadians who would make a far better Commissioner of the CFL would probably more than fill up respective football stadiums in each Canadian city. *Mr. Ambrosie, do the CFL a favour and please resign if you have any respect for OUR GAME!*

Reference: *Wikipedia.*

CHAPTER 2

XFL: CFL's ultimate problem is a shortage of brains and not money

*L*ET'S FACE IT FOLKS. THE NFL's financial success was not something which dropped from the sky. The success of the NFL has been propelled by smart people[26] who have made smart decisions. Smart people making smart decisions has resulted in professional leagues across North America being able to face the challenge of the pandemic without selling out their identities.

It is more than apparent that the CFL is not run by smart people. A smart league run by a smart Commissioner would have used all that time wasted in seeking to obtain corporate welfare[27] from the Justin Trudeau government to instead pursue an "NFL playbook" for achieving success. Correspondingly, a smart league run by a smart Commissioner would not be kowtowing to a league like of the XFL with no games played, with no proven financial success, and with a paper trail of failure.

A smart league run by a smart Commissioner would have been inspired by the smart people running the NFL. Such smart people would have made sure that the CFL's financial survival would not become dependent on stadium ticket sales.

A smart league run by a smart Commissioner would have seen the pandemic as a wake-up call and would have gone into hyper-drive to raise money for the CFL from the kind of corporate branding strategy that has assured the NFL a diversity of financial revenue streams. Indeed, money from ticket sales is a relatively small portion of the NFL's financial revenue.

The average Canadian football fan would be hard pressed to find any kind of CFL branded merchandise, unlike the seemingly endless NFL[28] products available. That's because the operation of the CFL is stuck in the 1970s.

I would gladly buy CFL T-shirts, along with other accessories and products with the CFL on it, or with a logo from a CFL team that I support, like the Toronto Argonauts. So would the millions of Canadians who watch Canadian football games on TV. Just imagine the millions of dollars of revenue the CFL has missed by never figuring this out.

I would furthermore add that I am also sure there are many American CFL fans who watch the games on ESPN who would love to also wear and buy products with CFL insignia just to mystify their NFL-supporting American brethren.

Unfortunately for such Canadian football fans, everything that the CFL has done during the pandemic betrays the fact that the CFL is apparently run by Tweedledum and

Tweedledee.[29] First, they fenced out players [30] from a discussion on a financial solution to the League's woes. Then, Chief Commissioner Randy Ambrosie wasted months and months shedding crocodile tears in front of Parliament on an appeal to the national tradition of the league. And then, the utter skepticism of parliamentarians on the sincerity of this Commissioner is then confirmed when he is ready to sell out to a Hollywood cowboy from America, who has no proven success of running a sports team, let alone a league.

The CFL Commissioner was shamefully grovelling for handouts[31] during the height of the pandemic when many Canadians didn't have money to pay rent or to put food on the table. That was when a smart commissioner would have sought to encourage CFL players to support local pandemic initiatives in their communities while also pursuing new cross-marketing opportunities with Canada's leading corporations.

I wonder how many CFL warriors who are part of the silent majority of supporters of Canadian football are watching in horror and shock on a prospective assimilation and destruction of a league that has been instrumental to expressing the national unity of Canada.

It is unfortunate just how our Canadian football traditions are now being subverted by so-called Canadian sports pundits whose principal source of information is XFL-branded sites churning out fake news aimed at misleading Canadians on the true market value of the XFL.

The XFL and its so-called value are no more credible than the main character in the folktale the "Emperor's New

Clothes." Without a season under its belt, the market value of the XFL is just as invisible as the Emperor's suit. No business people with any brains would jump into bed and prostitute their soul to a league and the nation that it represents with no documented evidence of financial and market success.

Indeed, the dust of previous XFL failures haven't even settled yet. It has just recently surfaced that Oliver Luck, the current CEO of the XFL, is still legally fighting with Vince McMahon[32] who was in charge of the former XFL. But just yesterday, yahoos representing XFL branded sites were criticizing me for stating that much of the news about the XFL outside of their branded sites has been negative, and the latest revelations further proves my point about the XFL.

And just for the record, I did try to watch a few XFL games at the start of its season while that league was being run by McMahon.

You might wonder, who is this guy writing these articles anyway? I am an alumnus of the top Business School in the nation. I successfully predicted that Target Canada was going to implode and have to retreat back into the United States[33] one year before it actually happened during a time when all the other journalists painted a rosy picture for the future of Target in Canada.

Stay tuned for my next article in which I discuss the huge risks for the CFL in damaging its credibility with its existing American fan base by jumping into bed with an unproven league that, in my view, is destined for a failure far worse than the previous XFL.

CHAPTER 3

CFL: Canadian sports journalists spread fake news fanfare over XFL

M ANY CANADIAN SPORTS JOURNALISTS WOULD have us believe that the XFL and The Rock have put in place a veritable marketing machine in America. All the CFL needs to do is tap in to that marketing machine for cash to rain down from the skies as a result of legions of American fans on the edge of their seats in anticipation for the XFL to begin, *so the story goes.*

But it doesn't take much research to figure out that all these Canadian sports journalists who are talking up a storm about the prospective benefits of a "CFL-XFL" merger are all responsible for shamelessly spreading fake news.

Have you checked Google News? It is pretty clear that the XFL is already well on its way to becoming a marketing flop.

It seems that 90% of talk about the XFL in the American media is coming from the XFL press box itself, and the 10%

of mass media banter about the XFL in America that is not from the XFL itself is not flattering.[40]

Most of the XFL's "good press" in the mass media is not coming from excited American sports journalists, but instead from idiotic Canadian sports journalists who haven't yet figured out that American sports pundits, and much of America outside of The Rock's head, *doesn't give a flying fu-k about the XFL!*

It is clear that The Rock has not been able to generate any real positive anticipation about the XFL in the United States. American football fans care about the NFL, U.S. college football, and the teams they have followed since time immemorial. *Heck,* the XFL is not even a match for the popularity of local American high school football.

Canadian football fans who are now salivating at The Rock are all the victims of fake news that Canadian sports journalists have been all too willing to deliver courtesy of an XFL propaganda machine directed north of the border and greedy big shots connected with the CFL front office.

The XFL has been an absolute marketing flop in America, and the XFL promises to take down the CFL with it in a stench of fake news spread by irresponsible Canadian sports journalists.

CFL: Saving Canadian Football is not rocket science

Professional sports leagues across North America have proven that where there's a will there's a way in efforts to face the challenges of the pandemic.

Unfortunately, CFL Commissioner Randy Ambrosie and the big shots he represents seem to be more focused on getting handouts than making the kind of adjustments other professional leagues have made successfully.

After failing to win a corporate welfare cheque from Prime Minister Justin Trudeau[34] these big shots now hope that The Rock will be their saviour. Never mind the fact that the typical American football fan, having had their fill of entertaining football from the NFL and NCAA college football, are probably more likely to pay attention to Bozo the Clown than the XFL's Hollywood-orchestrated shitshow.

Mention the XFL to the average American football fan and you will likely get laughter shortly afterwards: *"Ha, ha, ha, that's not real football,"* or, *"You mean that league started by that pro wrestler? Ha, ha, ha!"*

The XFL has become a veritable butt of jokes among U.S. comedians.[35]

Do you remember the CFL back in 1971 when Leo Cahill ran the Toronto Argonauts? These were the days when Cahill would just walk around NFL lockerooms with a suitcase of money and plucked elite American football players like Joe Theismann at will. It was a time when the CFL had swagger over the NFL. Watch the documentary below if you don't believe me.[36] That is the kind of swagger that Canadian football fans and teams can regain if smarter heads prevail, rather than the incompetence from within the upper management that is at the core of the CFL's problems and sought short-sighted XFL solution.

Here's the simple solution to getting the over 100-year-old Canadian professional football tradition back on track.

The big shots[37] and the Canadian Football League Players Association[38] (CFLPA) should first come together and pick a mutually agreeable auditor who will then reveal to all CFLPA management just how much money there is available for each CFL team playing the season from existing TV contracts with Canadian broadcasters,[39] ESPN,[40] and from other potential sources.

The CFLPA could then discuss with each group of players on each team the financial constraints, then determine which players are prepared to make some financial sacrifices to play and which would prefer to play when there is more money available.

The CFLPA would then provide its report to the big shots on each team.

The CFL big shots would then hold an emergency draft from the U-Sports[41] Canadian university football players to fill in temporary positions for players who want to sit out the season because they do not want to make the financial sacrifice. The jobs of the regular CFL players would be protected with a clause stipulating that should they change their mind, then the job is theirs.

The same emergency draft would also be to replace any American players who would not be able to play in Canada because of Canadian pandemic quarantine rules.

Such a solution would protect Canadian football and provide needed practice to Canadian university football players who would likely be very enthusiastic about playing football in the majors and with a salary.

The XFL has just about as must traction in the United States as a Hollywood B-movie. The last time the CFL flirted with American expansion and the allure of alleged U.S. TV market dollars under Larry Smith,[42] it almost resulted in the death of the CFL. The money being dangled in front of the CFL's bigshot Board of Governors is little more than fool's gold.

The CFL's success among Canadian fans and its international fan base which includes Americans is its uniqueness, our national tradition and its overall substance which are all totally lacking in the XFL.

Those short-sighted yahoos who are getting excited about a merger with the XFL and all that American cash are dreaming in technicolour.

If the CFL jumps in with the XFL, you can expect that it will destroy itself when the XFL begins to implode, when American football fans have had enough laughs after one or two games if the XFL eventually gets that far.

Have you checked Google News? It is pretty clear that the XFL is already well on its way to becoming a marketing flop. It seems that 90% of talk about the XFL in the American media is coming from the XFL press box itself, and the 10% of mass media banter about the XFL in America that is not from the XFL itself is not flattering.[40]

Most of the XFL's "good press" is not coming from excited American sports journalists, but instead from idiotic Canadian sports journalists who haven't yet figured out that American sports pundits, and much of America outside of The Rock's head, *doesn't give a flying fu-k about the "XFL"!*

I compare the XFL to a street pimp dangling a carrot in front of a prospective street prostitute. In The Rock's efforts to exploit the credibility of the CFL for his own self-serving ends, he will take down the CFL with it when the XFL surely implodes once again, but only if Canadian football fans allow them to do it.

If you like this solution, circulate it to as many Canadian football fans and owners you know and let's get Canadian football back on track and rescued from the XFL shitshow. Save Canadian football from Ambrosie's bromance with "The Rock."

CFL-XFL merger would damage Canadian football

T HERE IS NO QUESTION THAT the Canadian football League has an established history as well as established prestige. Decades ago, a former owner of the Toronto Argonauts used to walk right into NFL locker rooms and sign big NFL names such as Joe Theismann to the CFL.[43]

The Canadian Football League has amassed some success under current commissioner Randy Ambrosie who has started to make tremendous strides with regard to expanding the league internationally. The promotional plan, entitled *CFL 2.0*,[44] would see Ambrosie forming strategic partnerships with leagues such as the Promotional American Football League of Mexico in order to promote player development.[45]

Additionally, the CFL made aggressive moves to partner with other professional football leagues in Europe. They partnered with leagues such as the German Football League as well as the football leagues in Austria and Italy.[46] [47] [48]

By the beginning of last year, the CFL had established partnerships with thirteen different leagues worldwide.[49] Then they built on its global movement by partnering with the Japanese X League.[50] The Canadian brand of football was gaining momentum around the world.

With all these considered and successful partnership, it is mind-boggling why the CFL would consider merging with a league with no overall track record of success.

I can safely say that a merger between the CFL and the XFL would be a huge detriment to the Canadian Football brand. There is no conceivable reason why the CFL would benefit from a partnership with a league that has crashed and burned on two separate occasions.

Many of us do not need to be reminded of the colossal failure in 2001 of the original XFL league that was founded by WWE chairman Vince McMahon and NBC executive Dick Ebersol. The XFL attempted to differentiate itself by offering camera views at innovative angles and by doing pro-wrestling related gimmicks that simply did not work on television. The ratings plunged. Soon after, the league folded. As a result, Vince McMahon and Dick Ebersol would lose a total of 70 million dollars combined.[51]

In 2018, Vince McMahon tried to bring back the XFL. He vowed that the league would look a lot different this time. The league would consist of eight teams and have a 10-game schedule.[52] After a promising opening week in terms to ratings, viewership declined rapidly fell off in the following weeks.[53]

One month after the beginning of the XFL season, the XFL canceled all remaining games due to the COVID-19 pandemic. Shortly thereafter, the XFL shut down all its operations and filed for Chapter 11 bankruptcy. The league stated that the COVID-19 pandemic has cost them millions of dollars in revenue.[54] Eventually, the league was put up for sale.

So, to summarize, the XFL failed on a colossal level in its 1st go-round. In the league's 2nd attempt, the XFL was not even able to get off the ground before the COVID-19 pandemic finished them off. The XFL was still in the start-up phase. Thus, the league had little to no revenue and no cash flow history to withstand the storm of COVID-19. It was reminiscent of a hurricane destroying a house with no foundation.

In August 2020, the XFL was sold for 15 million dollars to a group led by actor Dwayne "The Rock" Johnson and his business partner.[55] Originally, the XFL was supposed to have a regular season in 2022. However, they have recently decided to postpone the season.[56] Based on the track record, the XFL is not even on the same planet as college football or the NFL in terms of relevancy in the U.S. The NCAA is a 4-billion-dollar business.[57] Even more impressively, the NFL brings in revenue that is as high as 16 billion dollars.[58]

Thus, the CFL's inexplicable decision to consider merging with the XFL is a strong signal that the league does not have a high opinion of its own legacy or ability. This potential action seems to play into the common misconception that the quality of play in the CFL is inferior to that of the NFL.

The CFL would be best served to enhance their business strategy by recognizing the awesome value that they possess. The recent COVID-19 pandemic should motivate the CFL to diversify its strategies with regards to earning revenue. There is no question that the CFL can earn more revenue by selling merchandise such as jerseys and t-shirts of fans favorite teams in local shops and supermarkets. The league can also be aggressive in terms of marketing strategies aimed toward attracting new and younger dans to the sport.

The CFL is more than just a league. The CFL fits into Canada's sports culture like a glove. A few years ago, a survey conducted by the Canada Project Survey found that 63% of respondents believed that the CFL was a key part of Canada's identity when it came to sports.

While hockey continues to hold the title as the #1 sport in Canada, the game of Canadian football is #2. This is due to the success of the CFL.

In light of this information, a merger with a worthless league such as the XFL would do permanent damage to the mystique of Canadian football. Rather than pin their hopes on an outside saviour like The Rock, the CFL would find greater success with more conviction about its worth and cultivating its own inherent value.

[1] Wikipedia contributors. (2020, December 8). "USA Basketball," Wikipedia, The Free Encyclopedia. Retrieved, April 27, 2021, from *https://en.wikipedia.org/w/index.php?title=USA_Basketball&oldid=993057912.*

[2] Wikipedia contributors. (2021, April 3). "Reebok," Wikipedia, The Free Encyclopedia. Retrieved April 27, 2021, from *https://en.wikipedia.org/w/index.php?title=Reebok&oldid=1017617423.*

[3] Wikipedia contributors. (2020, December 4). "1956 in Canadian football," Wikipedia, The Free Encyclopedia. Retrieved April 27, 2021, from *https://en.wikipedia.org/w/index.php?title=1956_in_Canadian_football&oldid=992363909.*

[4] Wikipedia contributors. (2020, June 4). "1967 CFL season," Wikipedia, The Free Encyclopedia. Retrieved April 27, 2021, from *https://en.wikipedia.org/w/index.php?title=1967_CFL_season&oldid=960710729.*

[5] Wikipedia contributors. (2021, January 15). "45th Grey Cup," Wikipedia, The Free Encyclopedia. Retrieved April 27, 2021, from *https://en.wikipedia.org/w/index.php?title=45th_Grey_Cup&oldid=1000590111.*

[6] Wikipedia contributors. (2021, March 26). "51st Grey Cup," Wikipedia, The Free Encyclopedia. Retrieved April 27, 2021, from *https://en.wikipedia.org/w/index.php?title=51st_Grey_Cup&oldid=1014413592.*

[7] Wikipedia contributors. (2021, March 27). "53rd Grey Cup," Wikipedia, The Free Encyclopedia. Retrieved April 27, 2021, from *https://en.wikipedia.org/w/index.php?title=53rd_Grey_Cup&oldid =1014466810*.

[8] Wikipedia contributors. (2021, March 25). "55th Grey Cup," Wikipedia, The Free Encyclopedia. Retrieved April 24, 2021, from *https://en.wikipedia.org/w/index.php?title=55th_Grey_Cup&oldid =1014134090*.

[9] Wikipedia contributors. (2021, April 22). "Rogers Communications," Wikipedia, The Free Encyclopedia. Retrieved April 27, 2021, from *https://en.wikipedia.org/w/index.php?title=Rogers_ Communications&oldid=1019222199*.

[10] Wikipedia contributors. (2021, April 20). "Premier of Ontario," Wikipedia, The Free Encyclopedia. Retrieved April 25, 2021, from *https://en.wikipedia.org/w/index.php?title=Premier_ of_Ontario&oldid=1018923437*.

[11] Wikipedia contributors. (2021, March 14). "Bill Davis," Wikipedia, The Free Encyclopedia. Retrieved April 27, 2021, from *https://en.wikipedia.org/w/index.php?title=Bill_Davis&oldid =1012152169*.

[12] Wikipedia contributors. (2021, February 24). "Principal Secretary (Canada)," Wikipedia, The Free Encyclopedia. Retrieved April 27, 2021, from *https://en.wikipedia.org/w/index.php?title= Principal_Secretary_(Canada)&oldid=1008721367*.

[13] Wikipedia contributors. (2021, April 7). "Acid rain," Wikipedia, The Free Encyclopedia. Retrieved April 27, 2021, from *https://en.wikipedia.org/w/index.php?title=Acid_rain&oldid =1016581947*.

[14] Wikipedia contributors. (2021, April 17). "1962 Canadian federal election," Wikipedia, The Free Encyclopedia. Retrieved

April 27, 2021, from *https://en.wikipedia.org/w/index.php?-title=1962_Canadian_federal_election&oldid=1018379741.*

[15] Wikipedia contributors. (2021, April 17). "1963 Canadian federal election," Wikipedia, The Free Encyclopedia. Retrieved April 27, 2021, from *https://en.wikipedia.org/w/index.php?-title=1963_Canadian_federal_election&oldid=1018380023.*

[16] Wikipedia contributors. (2021, April 17). "1965 Canadian federal election," Wikipedia, The Free Encyclopedia. Retrieved April 27, 2021, from *https://en.wikipedia.org/w/index.php?-title=1965_Canadian_federal_election&oldid=1018362151.*

[17] Wikipedia contributors. (2021, April 22). "Lester B. Pearson," Wikipedia, The Free Encyclopedia. Retrieved April 27, 2021, from *https://en.wikipedia.org/w/index.php?title=Lester_B._Pearson&oldid=1019276551.*

[18] Wikipedia contributors. (2021, April 22). "Pierre Trudeau," Wikipedia, The Free Encyclopedia. Retrieved April 27, 2021, from *https://en.wikipedia.org/w/index.php?title=Pierre_Trudeau&oldid=1019309252.*

[19] Wikipedia contributors. (2021, April 19). "John Turner," Wikipedia, The Free Encyclopedia. Retrieved April 27, 2021, from *https://en.wikipedia.org/w/index.php?title=John_Turner&oldid=1018719758.*

[20] Wikipedia contributors. (2021, January 14). "Torys," Wikipedia, The Free Encyclopedia. Retrieved April 27, 2021, from *https://en.wikipedia.org/w/index.php?title=Torys&oldid=1000356980.*

[21] Wikipedia contributors. (2020, April 9). "Davies Ward Phillips & Vineberg," Wikipedia, The Free Encyclopedia. Retrieved April 27, 2021, from *https://en.wikipedia.org/w/index.php?title=Davies_Ward_Phillips_%26_Vineberg&oldid=949977292.*

[22] "Behind the world's most successful events," (2021). Retrieved April 26, 2021, from *https://www.audienceview.com/*.

[23] Wikipedia contributors. (2021, April 4). "CJCL," Wikipedia, The Free Encyclopedia. Retrieved April 27, 2021, from *https://en.wikipedia.org/w/index.php?title=CJCL&oldid=1015876422*.

[24] Wikipedia contributors. (2021, January 30). "Ted Workman," Wikipedia, The Free Encyclopedia. Retrieved April 27, 2021, from *https://en.wikipedia.org/w/index.php?title=Ted_Workman&oldid=1003656813*.

[25] Wikipedia contributors. (2021, March 26). "Canadian Football League in the United States," Wikipedia, The Free Encyclopedia. Retrieved April 27, 2021, from *https://en.wikipedia.org/w/index.php?title=Canadian_Football_League_in_the_United_States&oldid=1014268362*.

[26] "How the NFL became the most competitive league in all of sports," (n.d.). Bleacher Report. Retrieved April 25, 2021, from *https://bleacherreport.com/articles/1574285-how-the-nfl-became-the-most-competitive-league-in-all-of-sports*.

[27] "Five takeaways from CFL commissioner Randy Ambrosie's House of Commons testimony," (n.d.). Sporting News Canada. Retrieved April 25, 2021, from *https://www.sportingnews.com/ca/cfl/news/five-takeaways-from-cfl-commissioner-randy-ambrosies-house-of-commons-testimony/wwzwqluzngow10by985bzoemf*.

[28] "NFLShop Canada Gear, 2020 NFL Gear, NFL apparel & NFL Merchandise | NFLShop.ca," (n.d.). NFL Shop. Retrieved April 21, 2021, from *https://www.nflshop.ca/*.

[29] Wikipedia contributors. (2021, January 14). "Tweedledum and Tweedledee," Wikipedia, The Free Encyclopedia. Retrieved 17:55, April 25, 2021, from *https://en.wikipedia.org/w/index.php?title=Tweedledum_and_Tweedledee&oldid=1000344585*.

[30] "CFL players upset with lack of communication from league," (n.d.) Regina. Retrieved April 25, 2021, from *https://re-*

gina.ctvnews.ca/it-shows-a-lack-of-respect-cfl-players-upset-with-lack-of-communication-from-league-1.4987363.

[31] The Canadian Press. (2020, April 29). "Trudeau says federal officials in talks with CFL about $150M request," Retrieved April 26, 2021, from *https://www.cbc.ca/sports/football/cfl/cfl-financial-assistance-federal-government-trudeau-considering-1.5549289.*

[32] Lincoln, D. (2021, February 27). "Oliver Luck says Vince McMahon fired him from XFL for 'Sinister Purpose,'" Retrieved April 27, 2021, from *https://www.totalprosports.com/2021/02/27/oliver-luck-says-vince-mcmahon-fired-him-from-xfl-for-sinister-purpose/.*

[33] "Target Canada's strategy doomed from the start," The Canadian Business Daily. (2013, August 23). Retrieved April 27, 2021, from *https://www.agoracosmopolitan.com/news/headline_news/2013/08/23/6670.html?fb_comment_id=671351846226798_94879759.*

[34] "Trudeau says federal officials in talks with CFL about $150M request," (2020, April 29). Retrieved April 26, 2021, from *https://www.cbc.ca/sports/football/cfl/cfl-financial-assistance-federal-government-trudeau-considering-1.5549289.*

[35] "43 jokes by professional comedians!" (n.d.) JokeBlogger.com. Retrieved April 26, 2021, from *https://www.jokeblogger.com/hottopic/XFL.*

[36] "1971 Toronto Argos Argonauts Joe Theismann Leon McQuay Simmons Thornton Profit," (n.d.). YouTube. Retrieved April 26, 2021, from *https://www.youtube.com/watch?v=FZ7yCaM2CAY.*

[37] "CFL governors expected to be brought up to speed on Ottawa loan discussion," (n.d.). In CFJC Today Kamloops. Retrieved April 27, 2021, from *https://cfjctoday.com/2020/08/06/*

cfl-governors-expected-to-be-brought-up-to-speed-on-ottawa-loan-discussion/.

[38] CFLPA.com. (n.d.). "The Canadian Football League Players Association," Retrieved April 27, 2021, from *https://cflpa.com/.*

[39] "Why did the CFL rush to extend their TV deal with TSN?" (n.d.). 3DownNation. Retrieved April 26, 2021, from *https://3downnation.com/2020/03/02/why-did-the-cfl-rush-to-extend-their-tv-deal-with-tsn/.*

[40] "Ambrosie: renewed ESPN TV deal important to expand CFL fan base in US," (n.d.). 3DownNation. Retrieved April 26, 2021, from *https://3downnation.com/2019/01/14/ambrosie-renewed-espn-tv-deal-important-to-expand-cfl-fan-base-in-us/.*

[41] "Men's Football," (n.d.). In U SPORTS. Retrieved April 26, 2021, from *https://usports.ca/en/sports/football/m.*

[42] Wikipedia contributors. (2021, April 22). "Larry Smith (Canadian politician)," Wikipedia, The Free Encyclopedia. Retrieved April 27, 2021, from *https://en.wikipedia.org/w/index.php?title=Larry_Smith_(Canadian_politician)&oldid=1019370566.*

[43] "XFL: CFL's Ultimate Problem Is a Shortage of Brains and Not Money." Toronto Business Journal, 10 Apr. 2021, *www.tobj.ca/news/opinion/2021/04/10/2855-xfl-cfls-ultimate-problem-is-a-shortage-of-brains-and-not-money.html.*

[44] Ambrosie, Randy. "Randy's Word: Talking CFL 2.0." CFL.ca, 3 Oct. 2018, *www.cfl.ca/2018/10/03/randys-word-talking-cfl-2-0/.*

[45] "CFL Could Play Two Games in Mexico in 2019." TSN, 2 Nov. 2018, *www.tsn.ca/good-chance-cfl-plays-two-games-in-mexico-next-season-1.1202839.*

[46] "CFL Forms Strategic Partnership with German League | CBC Sports." CBC news, CBC/Radio Canada, 31 Jan. 2019, *www.cbc.ca/sports/football/cfl/cfl-forms-strategic-partnership-with-german-league-1.5000451.*

[47] "CFL Secures Partnership with the Austrian American Football Federation | CBC Sports." CBCnews, CBC/Radio Canada, 6 Feb. 2019, *www.cbc.ca/sports/football/cfl/cfl-partnership-austria-1.5008370.*

[48] "Italy Becomes 9th International Football League to Join Forces with CFL." Sportsnet.ca, Canadian Press, 20 Feb. 2019, *www.sportsnet.ca/football/cfl/italy-becomes-9th-international-football-league-join-forces-cfl/.*

[49] "CFL Reaches Co-Operative Partnership Agreement with Brazilian Federation." TSN, 21 Jan. 2020, *www.tsn.ca/cfl-reaches-co-operative-partnership-agreement-with-brazilian-federation-1.1430644.*

[50] Yokota, Takashi, and Hiroshi Ikezawa. "New CFL-X League Alliance Spans the Pacific." The Japan Times, 28 Dec. 2019, *www.japantimes.co.jp/sports/2019/12/28/more-sports/football/new-cfl-x-league-alliance-spans-pacific/.*

[51] "XFL Is Down for the Count." ABC News, 11 May 2001, *https://abcnews.go.com/Entertainment/story?id=105329&page=1.*

[52] Kercheval Feb 8, Ben. "XFL 2020 Viewer's Guide: Schedule, Players, Coaches Everything to Know about New Football League." CBSSports.com, 8 Feb. 2020, *www.cbssports.com/xfl/news/xfl-2020-viewers-guide-schedule-players-coaches-everything-to-know-about-new-football-league/.*

[53] Zucker, Joseph. "XFL's Week 4 Games Average 1.4M Viewers as Ratings Drop for 3rd Straight Week." Bleacher Report, Bleacher Report, 3 Mar. 2020, *https://bleacherreport.com/articles/2878993-xfls-week-4-games-average-14m-viewers-as-ratings-drop-for-3rd-straight-week.*

[54] "XFL Files For Bankruptcy, Lost '10s Of Millions' Due To COVID-19." TMZ, TMZ, 13 Apr. 2020, *www.tmz.com/2020/04/13/xfl-bankruptcy-league-fold-millions-lay-offs/.*

[55] Kerr Aug 3, Jeff. "Dwayne 'The Rock' Johnson Buys XFL for $15 Million with Partners RedBird Capital and Dany Garcia." CBSSports.com, 3 Aug. 2020, *www.cbssports.com/nfl/news/ dwayne-the-rock-johnson-buys-xfl-for-15-million-with-partners-redbird-capital-and-dany-garcia/*.

[56] Schad, Tom. "XFL Puts Plans for 2022 Season on Hold While Exploring Potential Partnership with CFL." USA Today, Gannett Satellite Information Network, 10 Mar. 2021, *www.usatoday. com/story/sports/xfl/2021/03/10/xfl-cfl-exploring-football-partner-ship-after-return-covid-19/6939886002/*.

[57] "College Football Is Now One Of The Big Sports Revenue Enterprises." Last Word on College Football, 21 Apr. 2021, *https://lastwordonsports.com/collegefootball/2021/04/16/how-college-football-became-a-4-billion-business/*.

[58] Colangelo, Michael. "The NFL Made Roughly $16 Billion in Revenue Last Year." USA Today, Gannett Satellite Information Network, 16 July 2019, *https://touchdownwire.usatoday. com/2019/07/15/nfl-revenue-owners-players-billions/*.